Dear Valentine Letters

MAD LIBS®

World's Greatest Word Game

By Roger Price and Leonard Stern

PSS!
PRICE STERN SLOAN

PRICE STERN SLOAN
Published by the Penguin Group
Penguin Group (USA) Inc., 375 Hudson Street, New York, New York 10014, U.S.A.
Penguin Group (Canada), 90 Eglinton Avenue East, Suite 700,
Toronto, Ontario, Canada M4P 2Y3
(a division of Pearson Penguin Canada Inc.)
Penguin Books Ltd, 80 Strand, London WC2R 0RL, England
Penguin Ireland, 25 St Stephen's Green, Dublin 2, Ireland
(a division of Penguin Books Ltd)
Penguin Group (Australia), 250 Camberwell Road, Camberwell, Victoria 3124, Australia
(a division of Pearson Australia Group Pty Ltd)
Penguin Books India Pvt Ltd, 11 Community Centre, Panchsheel Park, New Delhi - 110 017, India
Penguin Group (NZ), Cnr Airborne and Rosedale Roads, Albany,
Auckland 1310, New Zealand
(a division of Pearson New Zealand Ltd)
Penguin Books (South Africa) (Pty) Ltd, 24 Sturdee Avenue,
Rosebank, Johannesburg 2196, South Africa

Penguin Books Ltd, Registered Offices:
80 Strand, London WC2R 0RL, England

ISBN 0-8431-2088-6

7 9 10 8

INSTRUCTIONS

It's Valentine's Day. You've got valentines to give to all your friends and family, but you just don't know what to say or how to say it. Every time you put your pencil to the paper, you draw a blank. Well, we can help you write your valentines— and they'll be really goofy and funny. Here's how:

Inside this booklet are 21 Mad Libs. They are just like regular Mad Libs; only after you fill in the blanks you can literally—no joke— tear each one out and mail it or send it. But first things first . . .

Step 1 is to fill in the blanks. You can do this by yourself (don't peek at the whole letter, just write in the missing words). Or, you can complete these just like you would a regular Mad Libs— with help from a friend. First, choose a letter inside this book. Don't read the story. Your friend should call out: "Give me a noun," "Give me an adjective," or whatever the space asks for. Your friend should write down the words you say in the blank spaces. Then your friend can read the completed letter to you—and it's ready to send. There's an example of a partially completed Mad Libs on the back cover of this book.

Step 2 is to tear out the letter carefully, fold it at the marker lines (see diagram below), seal it with a Mad Libs sticker, and write the name of your valentine on the front! Then you can give, send, or mail the letter. (Remember to include your valentine's address if you're going to mail the letter. And don't forget a stamp!)

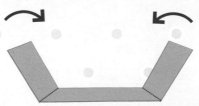

How Much I Love You

XOXO

Dear Love-_____,
            NOUN

My love is so _____ that it can hardly be
             ADJECTIVE

expressed in _____. It is higher than the
          PLURAL NOUN

highest _____, deeper than the deepest
        NOUN

_____, and as solid as a/an _____. I love
  NOUN   NOUN

you more than anyone in the whole _____
                          ADJECTIVE

world, even more than my stuffed _____. I
                         NOUN

cherish every _____ moment we're together.
           ADJECTIVE

Spending time with you is better than _____
                        VERB ENDING IN "ING"

at the mall or having a/an _____-over with
                    VERB

my best _____. It's even better than watching
      PLURAL NOUN

American _____ on TV! Please say you'll be my
            NOUN

_____ this Valentine's Day.
   NOUN

I'm _____ for you,
     ADJECTIVE

_____
       YOUR NAME

From DEAR VALENTINE LETTERS MAD LIBS® • Copyright © 2006 by Price Stern Sloan, a division of Penguin Young Readers Group, 345 Hudson Street, New York, New York 10014.

MAD LIBS

MAD LIBS

To:
_____
_____
_____

From:
_____
_____

xoxo

Dear Teacher

Dear Mr./Ms. _____,

TEACHER'S LAST NAME

Happy Valentine's Day to the best _____

NOUN

in the whole school! I like it when you teach us about

_____ and how to _____.

PLURAL NOUN   VERB

My favorite subject is _____ History.

ADJECTIVE

Your _____ enthusiasm for learning

ADJECTIVE

inspired me to research Valentine's Day. According to

the _____ I read, it all started with a/an

PLURAL NOUN

_____ named Saint _____

NOUN   NAME OF PERSON (MALE)

and a/an _____ love letter he wrote to

ADJECTIVE

a young _____. I'm sure you know all this

NOUN

because you know all kinds of _____ facts.

ADJECTIVE

Anyway, I don't want you to think I looked this up for

_____ credit—but I sure could use a/an

ADJECTIVE

_____ in class. What do you think?

LETTER OF THE ALPHABET

Your _____ student,

ADJECTIVE

_____

YOUR NAME

From DEAR VALENTINE LETTERS MAD LIBS® • Copyright © 2006 by Price Stern Sloan, a division of Penguin Young Readers Group, 345 Hudson Street, New York, New York 10014.

MAD LIBS

MAD&LIBS®

To: _____

_____

_____

From: _____

_____

Our Valentine's Date

Dear _____,
　　　　NAME OF PERSON

What are you doing after _____
　　　　　　　　　　　　　　　　NOUN

practice on Valentine's Day? Want to come over to my

_____? We can ride the school _____,
　　NOUN　　　　　　　　　　　　　　　　　　　NOUN

or, if it's a bright and _____ day, we can
　　　　　　　　　　　　　ADJECTIVE

_____. If you stay for dinner, you're in for
　　VERB

a/an _____ treat. My dad loves to barbecue
　　　　ADJECTIVE

prime _____. He is practically a gourmet
　　　　PLURAL NOUN

_____. His steaks are juicy, _____,
　　NOUN　　　　　　　　　　　　　　　　　　ADJECTIVE

and guaranteed to melt in your _____. And
　　　　　　　　　　　　　　　　PART OF THE BODY

my mom makes chocolate chip _____ that
　　　　　　　　　　　　　　　　　PLURAL NOUN

are out of this _____. You'll be eating them
　　　　　　　　　NOUN

until they come out your _____. After dinner
　　　　　　　　　　　PART OF THE BODY (PLURAL)

we can go to the movies. _____ *Impossible*
　　　　　　　　　　　　　　　NOUN

is playing. And, because it's Valentine's Day, I'll even pay

for the _____ popcorn.
　　　　ADJECTIVE

_____,
　　ADVERB

_____
　　YOUR NAME

From DEAR VALENTINE LETTERS MAD LIBS® • Copyright © 2006 by Price Stern Sloan, a division of Penguin Young Readers Group, 345 Hudson Street, New York, New York 10014.

MAD LIBS®

To: _____

From: _____

Dear Grandma

Dear Grandma,

Happy Valentine's Day! Mom says you're probably coming to visit us this weekend. I'll keep my _____ crossed. I love spending _____
PLURAL NOUN   ADJECTIVE

time with you. There's so much I want to do. I'd like you to meet my new _____ friends, and I
ADJECTIVE

can't wait to show you the _____ I made in
NOUN

_____ class. Most of all, I want you to meet
NOUN

our new pet _____. He's part-Labrador and
NOUN

part-_____. Gotta run. Mom's calling me for
NOUN

dinner. She's making macaroni and _____ and
NOUN

homemade mashed _____. They're good, but
PLURAL NOUN

never as good as yours.

Love and _____,
PLURAL NOUN

_____
YOUR NAME

MAD LIBS®

To:
_____
_____

From:
_____
_____

Place
Stamp
Here.

I Love You Because...

1. You've got so many good _____! You're
   PLURAL NOUN

   always willing to lend a helping _____ and
   PART OF THE BODY

   you always have a bright _____ on your face.
   NOUN

2. You tell me _____ jokes when I'm feeling
   ADJECTIVE

   down in the _____. You have the delivery of
   PLURAL NOUN

   a stand-up _____ and always make me laugh.
   NOUN

3. You are the definition of a true _____ friend.
   COLOR

   You're always there, through _____ or shine,
   NOUN

   through thick and _____.
   ADJECTIVE

4. You're a/an _____ optimist. Your cup is
   ADJECTIVE

   always half-_____.
   ADJECTIVE

Thanks for all the times you've turned my _____
   NOUN

upside down!

_____ yours,
ADVERB

_____
YOUR NAME

MAD LIBS

From DEAR VALENTINE LETTERS MAD LIBS® • Copyright © 2006 by Price Stern Sloan,
a division of Penguin Young Readers Group, 345 Hudson Street, New York, New York 10014.

MAD LIBS

To:

_____

_____

_____

From:

_____

_____

_____

Place Stamp Here.

Why I Hate Valentine's Day

Dear _____,
_____NAME OF PERSON_____

Don't you just hate Valentine's Day? Everyone has such

_____ expectations, and it's always such
____ADJECTIVE____

a/an _____ letdown. At least I think so. Maybe
____ADJECTIVE____

it's because I'm allergic to red _____, so
_____PLURAL NOUN_____

getting a dozen of them makes me _____
_____VERB_____

or break out in a cold _____. And don't
_____NOUN_____

even get me started on chocolate-covered

_____. I'm still stuffed from Halloween!
_____PLURAL NOUN_____

And I will *not* buy another _____ card with
_____ADJECTIVE_____

_____ pink _____ on the cover
____ADJECTIVE____   _____PLURAL NOUN_____

that says something _____ like: "Won't
_____ADJECTIVE_____

You Be My _____?"
_____NOUN_____

_____ Humbug to Valentine's Day!
_____SILLY WORD_____

_____,
_____ADVERB_____

_____
_____YOUR NAME_____

MAD☺LIBS®

To: _____

_____

_____

From: _____

_____

Place
Stamp
Here.

Have You Heard?

Dear _____,
<small>NAME OF PERSON</small>

You'll never guess what I just heard—_____
<small>NAME OF PERSON (MALE)</small>

is going to ask you to be his _____! Isn't
<small>NOUN</small>

that _____? I know your _____ must
<small>ADJECTIVE</small>   <small>NOUN</small>

be beating with excitement and you want to tell all

your _____, but you can't tell another living
<small>PLURAL NOUN</small>

_____. I gave my _____ word
<small>NOUN</small>   <small>ADJECTIVE</small>

to keep my _____ sealed. Oh, and guess
<small>PART OF THE BODY (PLURAL)</small>

what else? _____ told me she likes
<small>NAME OF PERSON (FEMALE)</small>

_____! It seems that love is in the
<small>NAME OF PERSON (MALE)</small>

_____ at _____ School this
<small>NOUN</small>   <small>CELEBRITY</small>

Valentine's Day! But please remember, if anyone asks

how you know, just say a little _____ told
<small>NOUN</small>

you. I don't want anyone to think that I _____
<small>VERB</small>

all over town spilling their _____. Believe
<small>PLURAL NOUN</small>

me, I know how to keep my _____ shut.
<small>NOUN</small>

Thanks,

_____
<small>YOUR NAME</small>

MADLIBS®

To: _____
_____
_____

From: _____
_____
_____

Place Stamp Here.

Friendly Valentine

Dear _____,
NAME OF PERSON

I know Valentine's Day is usually for _____
PLURAL NOUN

and_____, but it's also a time to celebrate
PLURAL NOUN

friendship. So I'm sending you this _____
ADJECTIVE

card just to say: "I'm glad you're my _____."
NOUN

I enjoy the _____ time we spend together.
ADJECTIVE

Especially ice-_____, playing video
VERB ENDING IN "ING"

_____ on your _____ TV, and
PLURAL NOUN ... ADJECTIVE

riding _____ around the block on the week-
PLURAL NOUN

ends. But, most of all, I enjoy our _____
ADJECTIVE

sleepovers when we stay up late watching old

_____, eating late-night _____,
PLURAL NOUN ... PLURAL NOUN

and sharing our innermost _____. Anyway,
PLURAL NOUN

have a/an _____ Valentine's Day today. I
ADJECTIVE

hope we stay best _____ for the rest of
PLURAL NOUN

our _____ lives!
ADJECTIVE

Keep it _____,
ADJECTIVE

_____
YOUR NAME

MAD LIBS®

From DEAR VALENTINE LETTERS MAD LIBS® • Copyright © 2006 by Price Stern Sloan,
a division of Penguin Young Readers Group, 345 Hudson Street, New York, New York 10014.

From: _____

_____

To: _____

_____

_____

Place Stamp Here.

MAD LIBS

Your Gift

Dear _____,
  NAME OF PERSON

I had such a difficult time picking out a Valentine's Day

_____ for you. First I thought a bouquet
  NOUN

of _____ would be just right, but then
  PLURAL NOUN

I remembered that you're _____. I didn't
  ADJECTIVE

want to make you _____. Then I saw a cute
  VERB

stuffed _____ that you could squeeze and
  NOUN

call _____, but you're too _____
  NAME OF PERSON   ADJECTIVE

for that sort of thing. I almost bought you a bottle of

the new perfume by _____, but when I
  CELEBRITY

sprayed a little on my _____, I almost
  PART OF THE BODY

passed out. It smelled like rotten _____!
  PLURAL NOUN

Finally, I found a really _____ gift for you—a
  ADJECTIVE

digital _____. Unfortunately, it cost an arm and
  NOUN

a/an _____, so you'll just have to settle for
  NOUN

this _____ card. I hope that every time you
  ADJECTIVE

read it you think of me, your old _____!
  NOUN

Hugs, kisses, and _____,
  PLURAL NOUN

_____
  YOUR NAME

MAD☺LIBS®

To:

_____

_____

_____

From:

_____

_____

_____

Place
Stamp
Here.

Roses Are Red

Dear _____,
NAME OF PERSON

_____ are red
PLURAL NOUN

_____ are blue
PLURAL NOUN

You love me and

I love _____!
PLURAL NOUN

Roses are _____
ADJECTIVE

Violets are _____
ADJECTIVE

Sugar is _____
ADJECTIVE

And so are you!

Roses are red

Violets are blue

_____ is fun
VERB ENDING IN "ING"

Especially with you!

_____,
ADVERB

_____
YOUR NAME

From DEAR VALENTINE LETTERS MAD LIBS® • Copyright © 2006 by Price Stern Sloan, a division of Penguin Young Readers Group, 345 Hudson Street, New York, New York 10014.

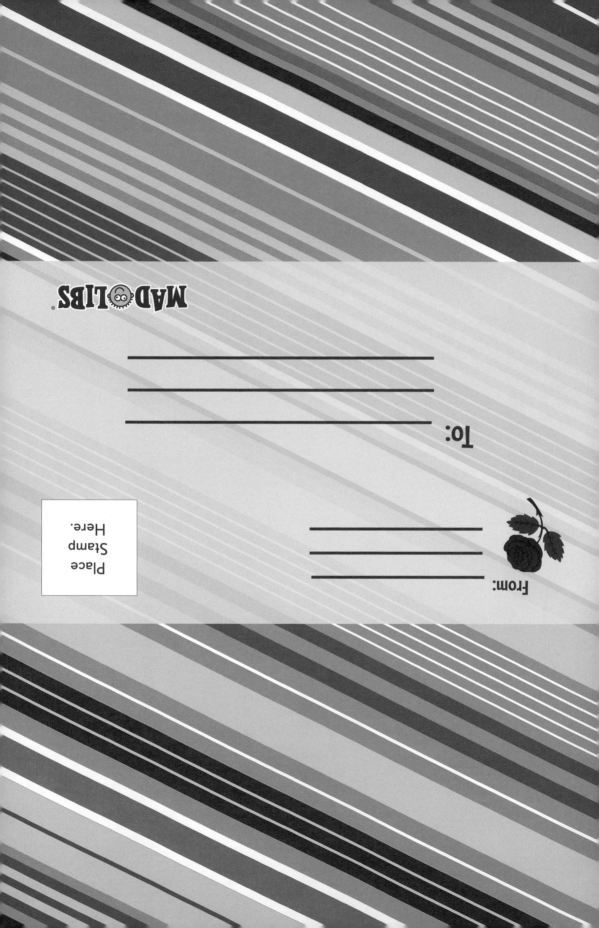

Dear Sister

Dear _____,
SISTER'S NAME

Having you as a sister means I always have

someone by my _____ who I can count on
NOUN

in _____ moments—as well as a/an _____
ADJECTIVE   NOUN

to talk to and a/an _____ to lean on.
PART OF THE BODY

Throughout our _____ lives, we
ADJECTIVE

have shared both laughter and _____.
PLURAL NOUN

I'm truly fortunate to have someone as loving and

_____ as you in my life. You're my
ADJECTIVE

_____ when I need help, my _____
OCCUPATION   OCCUPATION

when I need advice, and my _____ when
OCCUPATION

I need _____. Who could ask for a
PLURAL NOUN

better _____ than you? Thank you for being my
NOUN

_____ sister and have a/an _____
ADJECTIVE   ADJECTIVE

Valentine's Day. (By the way, I borrowed your

_____. You don't mind, do you? Thanks!)
PLURAL NOUN

Forever your _____,
NOUN

_____
YOUR NAME

From DEAR VALENTINE LETTERS MAD LIBS® • Copyright © 2006 by Price Stern Sloan, a division of Penguin Young Readers Group, 345 Hudson Street, New York, New York 10014.

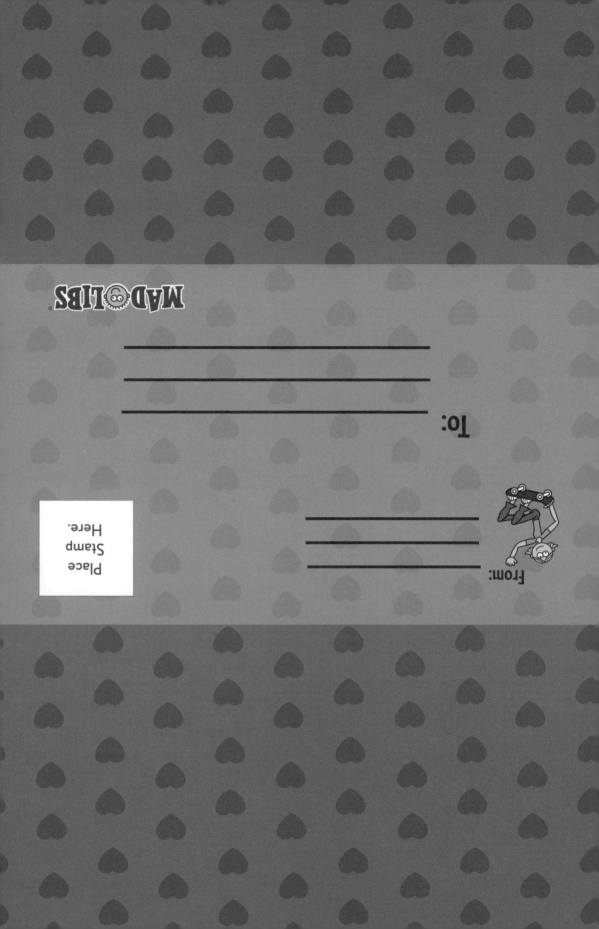

MAD LIBS®

To: _____
_____
_____

From: _____
_____

Dear Dad

Dear Dad,

Some fathers coach their kids' _____
NOUN

teams. Some fathers take their kids on trips to

exotic _____. Some fathers _____
PLURAL NOUN   VERB

morning, noon, and night. Of all the different kinds of

_____ dads, I have the best one! You're
ADJECTIVE

funny, caring, and _____. You wake me up in
ADJECTIVE

the morning and tuck me into my _____
NOUN

at night. You help me with my reading, writing, and

_____ homework. They should call you
VERB ENDING IN "ING"

"_____ Dad!" When I grow up, I want to
ADJECTIVE

_____ just like you. Thank you for being
VERB

the world's best _____, and Happy
NOUN

Valentine's Day!

Your _____,
NOUN

_____
YOUR NAME

P.S. Can you raise my allowance to _____ dollars
NUMBER

a week? Thanks!

MADLIBS®

To:
_____
_____
_____

From:
_____
_____

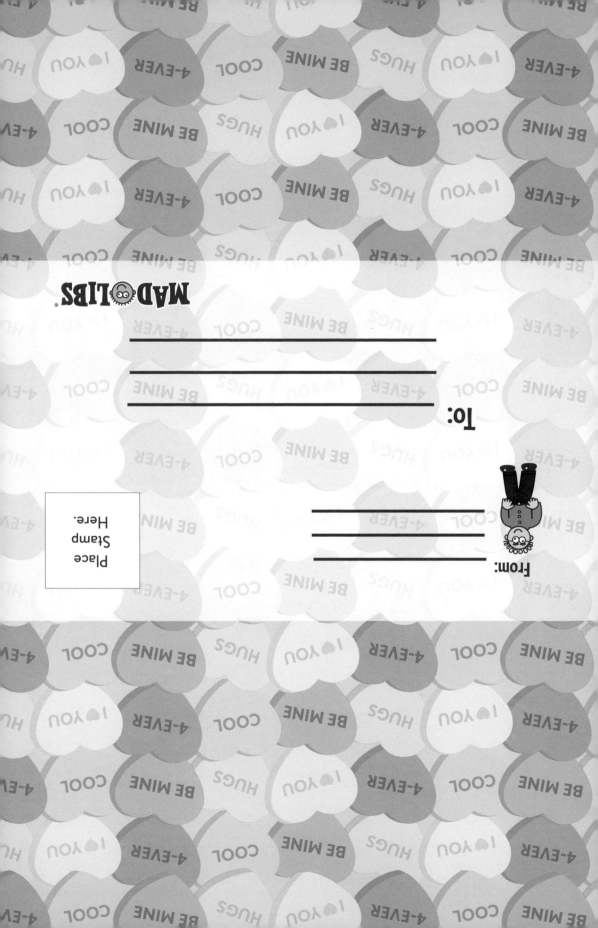

Place
Stamp
Here.

Secret Admirer

Dear _____,
      NAME OF PERSON

I would like to tell you face to _____
                                 PART OF THE BODY

how _____ I think you are, but I'm
     ADJECTIVE

_____ shy, so I'm sending you this letter
 ADVERB

instead. I sometimes look at you during Mr./Ms.

_____ class. I just love the way you drum
 TEACHER'S LAST NAME

your _____ on the desk and bite your
      PLURAL NOUN

_____ as you listen. The other day
 PART OF THE BODY

while I was collecting our _____ tests on
                           ADJECTIVE

_____ and Juliet, I looked at your hand-
 NAME OF PERSON

writing and noticed you dot your I's with little

_____. That's so _____! I wish
 PLURAL NOUN   ADJECTIVE

I had the courage to call you or _____
                                 VERB

with you in the cafeteria, but I don't. So this is my

_____ way of telling you that you have a
 ADJECTIVE

secret _____. Happy Valentine's Day.
       NOUN

Your Secret Admirer

From DEAR VALENTINE LETTERS MAD LIBS® • Copyright © 2006 by Price Stern Sloan, a division of Penguin Young Readers Group, 345 Hudson Street, New York, New York 10014.

MAD LIBS®

To: _____

_____

_____

From: _____

_____

4-EVER

Dear Brother

Dear _____,
BROTHER'S NAME

Even though I still don't forgive you for putting a live

_____ in my bed and scaring me out of my
NOUN

_____, and even though I still don't forgive
PLURAL NOUN

you for using my _____ dolls as crash-test
ADJECTIVE

dummies in your remote-controlled _____, and
NOUN

even though I still don't forgive you for chasing me all

over the house with that slimy _____, I still wish
NOUN

you a/an _____ Valentine's Day. And in the spirit
ADJECTIVE

of the holiday, I should tell you that when you're not

_____ around like a/an _____,
VERB ENDING IN "ING"   NOUN

you can be a pretty darn _____ brother.
ADJECTIVE

You can also be quite _____ in your own
ADJECTIVE

way, and it's not really so _____ having you
ADJECTIVE

around. Sometimes.

Later, _____,
NOUN

_____
YOUR NAME

From DEAR VALENTINE LETTERS MAD LIBS® • Copyright © 2006 by Price Stern Sloan, a division of Penguin Young Readers Group, 345 Hudson Street, New York, New York 10014.

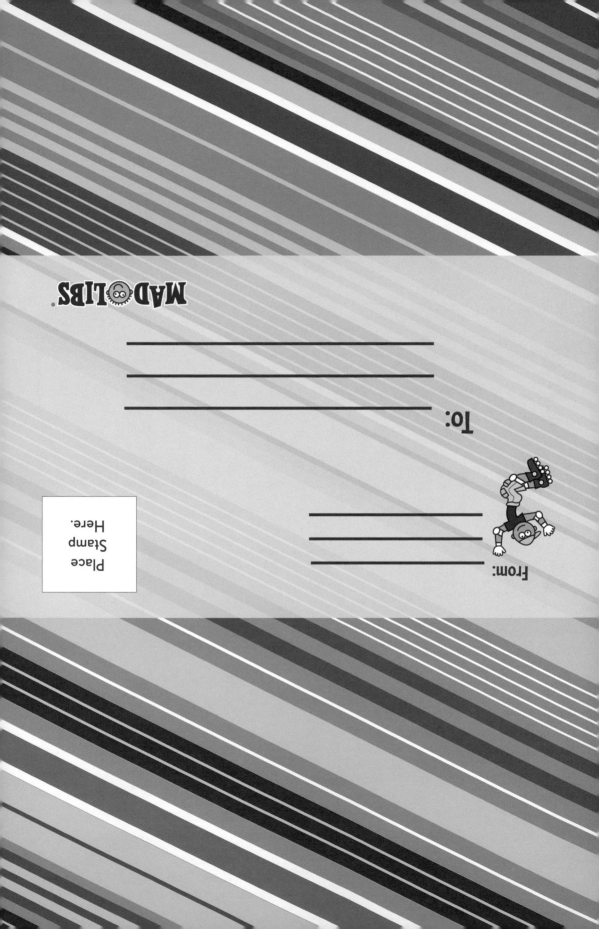

MAD LIBS®

To: _____
_____
_____

From: _____
_____

Place
Stamp
Here.

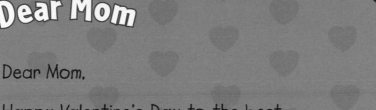

Dear Mom

Dear Mom,

Happy Valentine's Day to the best _____ in
NOUN

the whole, _____ world! You're the prettiest,
ADJECTIVE

smartest, and nicest _____ I know. You're
NOUN

also a/an _____ cook who makes the best
ADJECTIVE

baked _____ this side of _____. Lots
PLURAL NOUN   A PLACE

of kids don't appreciate their _____, but I
PLURAL NOUN

sure do. You always have the right _____ for my
PLURAL NOUN

_____ questions. And have I mentioned how
ADJECTIVE

_____ you are? You have a face that ought
ADJECTIVE

to be on _____ covers. Your name ought
NOUN

to be in _____ on Broadway! People should
PLURAL NOUN

read about you in a/an _____ magazine! Is
NOUN

now a good time to tell you I accidentally broke your

favorite _____?
NOUN

As _____ as the day I was born,
ADJECTIVE

_____
YOUR NAME

From DEAR VALENTINE LETTERS MAD LIBS® • Copyright © 2006 by Price Stern Sloan,
a division of Penguin Young Readers Group, 345 Hudson Street, New York, New York 10014.

Valentine's Day Dance

Hey, _____,
     NAME OF PERSON

Are you going to the Valentine's Day _____
                                           NOUN

this weekend? It should be really _____.
                                       ADJECTIVE

There'll be a live _____ playing music, and
                        NOUN

the gym will be decorated like an underwater

_____! There will be _____
      NOUN   PLURAL NOUN

on the walls and _____ hanging from
                     PLURAL NOUN

the ceiling. The only drag is that we have to wear

our bathing _____ or scuba _____.
               PLURAL NOUN   PLURAL NOUN

It sure would be _____ to see you there.
                      ADJECTIVE

I'll save a dance for you but only if it's not too

_____. I'm known to have two left
     ADJECTIVE

_____.
   PLURAL NOUN

Looking forward to _____ with you,
                        VERB ENDING IN "ING"

_____
   YOUR NAME

MAD LIBS

To:
_____
_____

From:
_____
_____

Place Stamp Here.

A Rose Is a Rose

Dear _____,
NAME OF PERSON

You're probably wondering why I'm not giving you a

red _____ today. Well, different colored
NOUN

roses all have their own _____ meanings.
ADJECTIVE

A red rose expresses passion, such as: "I've fallen

_____ over _____ in love
PART OF THE BODY   PLURAL NOUN

with you." The pink rose means gentleness and

_____ happiness as in: "Let's go
ADJECTIVE

_____ and buy some new _____!"
VERB ENDING IN "ING"   PLURAL NOUN

Yellow symbolizes the hope of _____ things
ADJECTIVE

to come. A white rose speaks of purity and innocence.

It is _____ rare. I just don't know which
ADVERB

color means: "I like _____with you. Let's
VERB ENDING IN "ING"

be best _____." That's just what I want
PLURAL NOUN

to say to you this Valentine's Day.

With love and _____,
PLURAL NOUN

_____
YOUR NAME

From DEAR VALENTINE LETTERS MAD LIBS® • Copyright © 2006 by Price Stern Sloan, a division of Penguin Young Readers Group, 345 Hudson Street, New York, New York 10014.

MAD LIBS®

MAD LIBS®

To: _____

From: _____

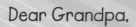
Dear Grandpa

Dear Grandpa,

Ever since I was just a little _____, Mom
                                    NOUN
has told me _____ stories about how you
                ADJECTIVE
and Grandma have celebrated Valentine's Day. Is it

true that one time you spelled out her name in

_____ on the front lawn and one year you
   PLURAL NOUN
put on a/an _____ costume and sang "My
                  NOUN
_____ Valentine" to her? And when you and
   ADJECTIVE
Grandma were _____, did you really walk
                    ADJECTIVE
_____ miles through a/an _____
   NUMBER   NOUN
storm and climb a very steep _____ just to
                                      NOUN
give her a handmade _____? And did you
                          NOUN
really tell her that you made it with all the love in your

_____? How _____ romantic—
PART OF THE BODY   ADVERB
I get _____ in my eyes whenever I think of
         PLURAL NOUN
that story. I love you, Gramps!

Your _____ grandkid,
        ADJECTIVE

_____
                YOUR NAME

From DEAR VALENTINE LETTERS MAD LIBS® • Copyright © 2006 by Price Stern Sloan,
a division of Penguin Young Readers Group, 345 Hudson Street, New York, New York 10014.

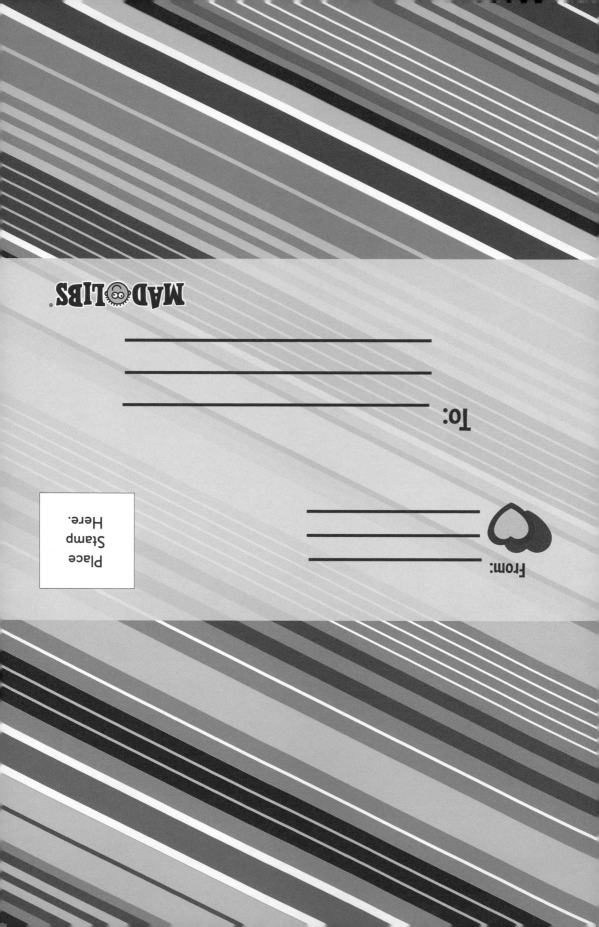

Dear Valentine

Dear _____,
NAME OF PERSON

If you want to be my valentine, here's what you must do.

1. When we see each other in the hallway, say,

   "_____!"
   SILLY WORD

2. Be _____ to my little _____.
   ADJECTIVE   NOUN

3. When we're on different _____-ball teams,
   VERB

   you have to let me _____.
   VERB

4. Tell your friends I'm the nicest _____
   NOUN

   you've ever met.

5. Sit with me at lunch. But don't talk with food in

   your _____ or eat with your _____.
   NOUN   PART OF THE BODY (PLURAL)

6. Whenever there's a school dance, you have to be my

   _____. And try to act _____-
   NOUN   ADJECTIVE

   don't spill punch all over your _____ or
         NOUN

   trip over your _____.
   PART OF THE BODY (PLURAL)

These are the rules. If you agree, sign below so I know

you _____ mean it.
ADVERB

Hugs and _____,
PLURAL NOUN

_____
YOUR NAME

 From DEAR VALENTINE LETTERS MAD LIBS® • Copyright © 2006 by Price Stern Sloan, a division of Penguin Young Readers Group, 345 Hudson Street, New York, New York 10014.

MAD@LIBS®

To:

_____

_____

_____

From:

_____

_____

_____

Candy Hearts

Dear _____,
　　　　　　　　　NAME OF PERSON

I have a hard time putting my _____ feelings
　　　　　　　　　　　　　　　　　　　　　ADJECTIVE

into words, so this Valentine's Day I thought I would get

these little candy _____ to do it for me.
　　　　　　　　　　　　PLURAL NOUN

But the messages are all too _____. They say
　　　　　　　　　　　　　　　　　ADJECTIVE

things like: "Sweetie" and "Hugs." *Boring!* I would like

candies that say: "Be_____!" "Sassy_____,"
　　　　　　　　　　　　ADJECTIVE　　　　　　　　　　　　　NOUN

or "_____ for Love!" Actually, I'd prefer a
　　　　ADJECTIVE

candy that has an even more _____ message
　　　　　　　　　　　　　　　　　　　ADJECTIVE

like: "When I think of you, it's like chocolate-covered

_____ raining down from the _____
　　PLURAL NOUN　　　　　　　　　　　　　　　　　　　PLURAL NOUN

while your _____ face lights up the night
　　　　　　　　ADJECTIVE

_____." I guess that wouldn't fit on a little
　　NOUN

piece of _____ though. So I'll just give you
　　　　　　　NOUN

a candy _____ that says "Hot _____"
　　　　　　　NOUN　　　　　　　　　　　　　　　　NOUN

on it. Hope it tastes as _____ as it looks!
　　　　　　　　　　　　　　　ADJECTIVE

Sweets for the _____,
　　　　　　　　　　ADJECTIVE

_____
　　　YOUR NAME

MAD LIBS

To:

_____

_____

_____

From:

_____

_____

Place
Stamp
Here.

The Day We Met

Dear _____,
<small>NAME OF PERSON</small>

I remember the first time I laid _____ on you.
<small>PLURAL NOUN</small>

You were seated at a/an _____ in the cafeteria,
<small>NOUN</small>

eating a/an _____-butter and jelly sandwich.
<small>NOUN</small>

The first thing I noticed was the way your _____
<small>NOUN</small>

shone in the sunlight. It was _____ at first sight.
<small>NOUN</small>

I carried my _____ over to your table, trying
<small>NOUN</small>

not to spill my cup of _____, and asked, "May I
<small>TYPE OF LIQUID</small>

_____ with you?" You smiled up at me, your
<small>VERB</small>

eyes like sparkling _____, and said, "Pull up
<small>PLURAL NOUN</small>

a/an _____." I was so excited that I spilled
<small>NOUN</small>

my drink all over your _____. I cried out,
<small>NOUN</small>

"Oh, _____!" Thank goodness you were so
<small>EXCLAMATION</small>

_____ about it. If you weren't, I'm sure we'd be
<small>ADJECTIVE</small>

celebrating this Valentine's Day with other _____!
<small>PLURAL NOUN</small>

Sweets and _____,
<small>PLURAL NOUN</small>

_____
<small>YOUR NAME</small>

From DEAR VALENTINE LETTERS MAD LIBS® • Copyright © 2006 by Price Stern Sloan, a division of Penguin Young Readers Group, 345 Hudson Street, New York, New York 10014.

MAD LIBS®

To: _____

_____

_____

From: _____

_____

_____

This book is published by

PSS!
PRICE STERN SLOAN

whose other splendid titles include such literary classics as

Letters from Camp Mad Libs®
Mad Libs® in Love
The Original #1 Mad Libs®
Son of Mad Libs®
Vacation Fun Mad Libs®
Winter Games Mad Libs®
Christmas Fun Mad Libs®
Graduation Mad Libs®
Monster Mad Libs®
You've Got Mad Libs®
Goofy Mad Libs®
Prime Time Mad Libs®
Slam Dunk Mad Libs®
Diva Girl Mad Libs®
Grab Bag Mad Libs®
Cool Mad Libs®
Dinosaur Mad Libs®
Mad Libs® from Outer Space
Kid Libs Mad Libs®
Haunted Mad Libs®
Off-the-Wall Mad Libs®
Mad Libs® On the Road
Mad Mad Mad Mad Mad Libs®
Straight "A" Mad Libs®
Upside Down Mad Libs®

and many, many more!